VIOLIN SOLOS ON SYMPHONY THEMES
VIOLIN SOLO PART
BY COSTEL PUSCOIU

FREE Piano Accompaniment download available online!
Visit: www.melbay.com/99981

MB99981

Visit us on the Web at www.melbay.com or www.billsmusicshelf.com

Contents

ABOUT THE AUTHOR

Costel Puscoiu was born on August 29, 1951, in Bucharest, Romania. He studied and graduated from the Ciprian Porumbescu College of Music in Bucharest, majoring in Composition and Theory. In Romania he worked as a music teacher, and for some years he was a conductor and researcher at the Institute for Ethnology and Folklore in Bucharest. He was also a member of the Society of Romanian Composers.

His compositions comprise symphonic music (symphonies, cantatas, concertos for viola), chamber music (string quartets, sonatas for clarinet and piano, contemporary pieces for several ensembles, music for pan flute), choir pieces, and film scores. His compositions are often influenced by Romanian folklore and Byzantine liturgies. He has also contributed to several musicological and folkloristic studies and articles.

In September of 1982 Puscoiu moved to the Netherlands from his native Romania; now he is working in the Music School department as a pan flute teacher and a leader of an orchestra at the Free Academy Westvest in Delft. Meanwhile he has become a member of the Dutch Composers Association.

Menuetto

(3rd Mouvement Theme from Symphony No. 92 "Oxford" in G Major)

Joseph Haydn
(1732 - 1809)

Allegro

(1st Mouvement Theme from Symphony No. 102 "With the Bagpipe" in D Major)

Joseph Haydn
(1732-1809)

Andante

(2nd Mouvement Theme from Symphony No. 94 "Surprise" in G Major)

Joseph Haydn
(1732 - 1809)

Molto Allegro

(1st Mouvement Theme from Symphony No. 40 in G Minor)

Wolfgang Amadeus Mozart
(1756 - 1791)

Andante
(2nd Mouvement Theme from Symphony No. 40 in G Minor)

Wolfgang Amadeus Mozart
(1756 - 1791)

Menuetto

(3rd Mouvement Theme from Symphony No. 41 "Jupiter" in G Major)

Wolfgang Amadeus Mozart
(1756 - 1791)

Allegro vivace

(1st Mouvement Theme from Symphony No. 41 "Jupiter" in C Major)

Wolfgang Amadeus Mozart

(1756 - 1791)

Marcia Funebre

(2nd Mouvement Theme from Symphony No. 3 "Eroica" in E flat Major)

Ludwig van Beethoven
(1770 - 1827)

Ode to Joy

(4th Mouvement Theme from Symphony No. 9 in D Minor)

Ludwig van Beethoven
(1770 - 1827)

Allegro con Brio

(1st Mouvement Theme from Symphony No. 5 in C Major)

Ludwig van Beethoven
(1770 - 1827)

Allegro con brio

Allegro ma non troppo

(1st Mouvement Theme from Symphony No. 6 "Pastoral" in F Major)

Ludwig van Beethoven
(1770 - 1827)

Allegro ma non troppo

p

f

f

p

f

Shepherd's Song

(5th Mouvement Theme from Symphony No.6 "Pastoral" in F Major)

Ludwig van Beethoven
(1770 - 1827)

Allegro Moderato

(1st Mouvement Theme from Symphony No. 8 "Unfinished" in B Minor)

Franz Schubert
(1797 - 1828)

Allegro Vivace

(1st Mouvement Theme from Symphony No. 4 "Italian" in A Major)

Felix Mendelssohn-Bartholdy
(1809 - 1847)

Scherzo

(3rd Mouvement Theme from Symphony No. 9 "Great" in C Major)

Franz Schubert
(1791 - 1828)

Romance

(2nd Mouvement Theme from Symphony No. 4 in D Minor)

Robert Schumann
(1810 - 1856)

Moderato

(3rd Mouvement Theme from Symphony No. 4 "Italian" in A Major)

Felix Mendelssohn-Bartholdy
(1809 - 1847)

Waltz

(2nd Mouvement Theme from "Symphony Fantastique") Hector Berlioz
(1803 - 1869)

Allegro non troppo

(1st Mouvement Theme from Symphony in D Minor)

César Franck
(1822 - 1890)

Allegro

(4th Mouvement Theme from Symphony No. 4 in C Minor)

Johannes Brahms
(1833 - 1897)

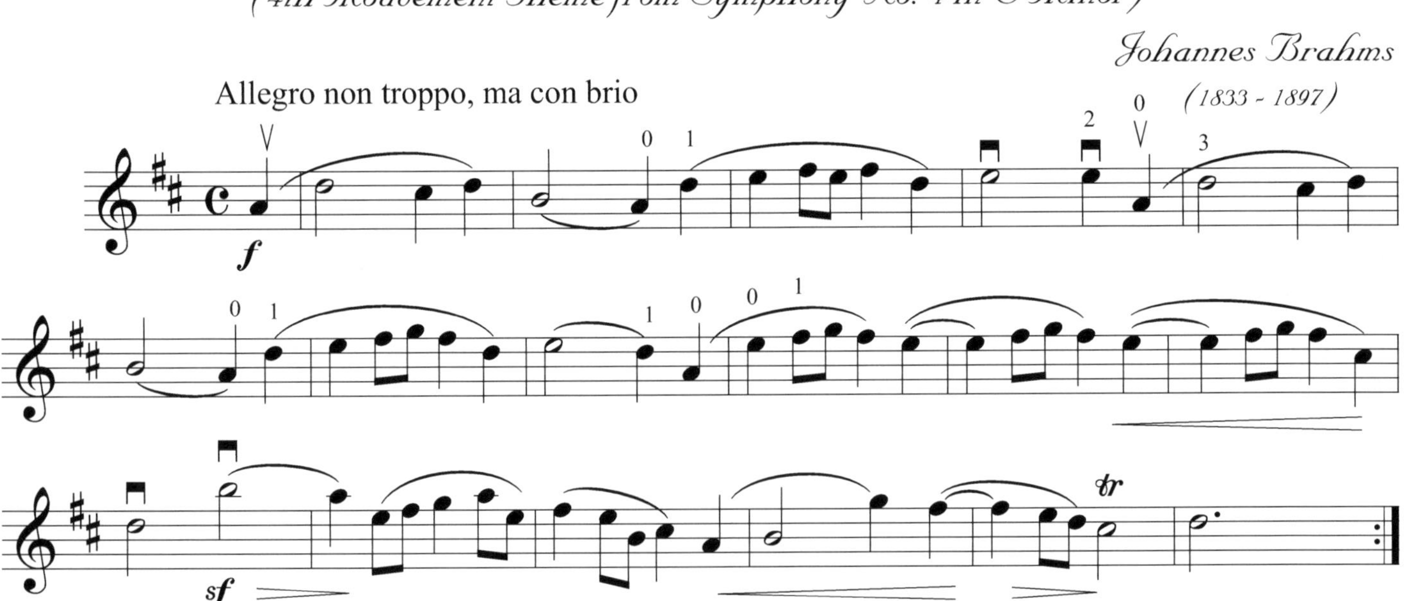

Allegretto Grazioso

(3rd Mouvement Theme from Symphony No. 2 in D Major)

Johannes Brahms
(1833 - 1897)

Allegretto grazioso (Quasi Andantino)

Poco Allegretto

(3rd Mouvement Theme from Symphony No. 3 in F Major)

Johannes Brahms
(1833 - 1897)

Allegro non troppo

(1st Mouvement Theme from Symphony No. 4 in E Minor)

Johannes Brahms
(1833 - 1897)

Allegretto Grazioso

(3rd Mouvement Theme from Symphony No. 8 in G Major)

Antonin Dvořák
(1841 - 1904)

Largo

(2nd Mouvement Theme from Symphony No.9 "From the New World" in E Minor)

Antonin Dvořák
(1841 - 1904)

Andante

(1st Mouvement Theme from Symphony No. 6 "Pathetique" in B Minor)

Andante Cantabile

(2nd Mouvement Theme from Symphony No. 5 in E Minor)

Piort Ilyitch Tchaikovsky
(1840 - 1893)

Allegro con Grazia

(2nd Mouvement Theme from Symphony No. 6 "Pathétique" in B Minor)

Piotr Ilyitch Tchaikovsky

(1840 - 1893)

Made in the USA
Monee, IL
07 July 2026

56551276R00017